Refle

Poems by Ruth Asch

With Artwork by James Tyldesley

To my beloved husband, Robert.

Published by
Saint Austin Press, London, 2009.
www.saintaustin.org

ISBN: 1 901157 46 6

Note

The poems in this collection are reflections: they are glances, images, of parts of the world and of life as I have seen them; and they are also in some sense, brief meditations on these phenomena. In both ways they are highly personal, even when purely imaginary; expressive responses which are neither meant nor should be taken as unqualified statements. I would not withdraw a syllable of the love expressed herein - but should be sorry if anyone were to take offence at rare scathing moments.

There are several very different styles of poem in this small book. This may seem inconsistent or confused enough to warrant some explanation: the choice of style in each case was an instinctive reaction to the subject matter and tone, either growing organically from an original inspiration or fitting into a known form. The sound of language has always been crucial to the experience and writing of poetry, which at its best is spoken music; for this reason I have, in some instances, opted for a rather old-fashioned style of English which, to my ear, has particular musical qualities - as well as if it felt more appropriate to the tone or subject matter.

It seemed to give a guiding form to group the collection thematically, though the titles are to be understood in their broadest sense. Within sections the arrangement often follows a line of thought or a natural development; but of course one reason for such a layout is to give the reader an advised choice - they need not be read from cover to cover. However they are read, I hope that in the wide variety of style and tone, and in the many glimpses of the world we share through another individual's eyes, every reader will find something to enjoy.

Table of Contents

Poems

Nature

Running after Rain 15
Salamanders....................................15
Puddles..15
Evening Walk....................................16
The Field 18
Reaction...20
Faux Pas...22
Ripening...23
Gnats..24
The Wind...24
First Thaw 26
A Window on the Night 27
Ablation 29
Musing on Trees..................................31
Before the Storm.................................32
La Petite Maine..................................33

Time and Change

Keys...39
Candle Lady 40
Time and Place 41
Adolescent.......................................43
Crush..43
Epiphany?..44
People of the Street.............................45
A Change...47
Infant's reaction to a doll......................47

Bratz 48
Chorleywood Lawn Cemetery 50
In Denial 52
Anthem of the Twentieth Century 54
To an Infant 55

Love and Friendship

To a Friend 61
Rebecca's Ring 62
Prodigal 63
Hidden Depths 65
Angel 67
Show 68
Innocent? 69
Untitled 70
Baptism by Fire 72
Your Eyes 73
Testimonial 74
Apologia 74
Love-Song 75
Betrayal 76
End of a Day 77
Womaniser 78
Tribute 79

Faith

Soul and Body 83
Birthday 86
The Abbey 87
Meditation watching the Sea 89
Such Terrible Humility 91
Song to my Soul 93
A Child 94
Rome 94

In Thanks 95
Journey 97
Liturgical Colours 97
Visitation 99
Patience 100
Lenten Songs I & II 101
Poem on Mass in the Kirks' chapel-like
dining room with furnishings rescued
from demolished old churches 103
Narcissus and his Followers 103
Simeon 107

Inspiration

Dreamland 111
A Walk in a state of Exhaustion 112
Books seen slipping to Sleep 113
A Secret Life 114
Insomniac 114
The Drunkard 116
Inspiration Unattained 116
Writer's Block /
Song of the Hermit-Crab Shell 118
Poetic Self 119
Looking Up 119
Looking Down 121
Personification 123
Like a Maple 125
A Sonnet to a Sonnet 126
Shadows 127
Untitled Sonnet 128
Appendix 129

Pictures

Waterfall 12
Trees 30
Tobias and the Angel 36
Mother and Child 58
Angel bearing Soul 66
Deposition 80
Woman with Skull and Mirror 92
Simeon and the Christchild 106
Woman Dreaming 108

Nature

Running After Rain

The motion! Arms and legs fast churning,
Soul free flying, hair free floating,
Swirling, passing visions swift in
Sparkling light – a filtered gold which
Flashes out in brighter shapes
At the water's greeting.
Dazzled in a shimmered prism-
World; flung flinging through a liquid-
Haze, as insubstantial as a
Dream – all flowed through me, rainwashed, swift:
In a mellow sea of honey-
Suckled air I dived.

Salamanders

Who could doubt the existence of fire-fish;
When walking a rainy, secret brimming lane
By night, they see the fire-rings silent splash
Through fathoms of a black street-lamp lit pool?

Puddles

In the trudging boot's mud-field below
The habit-wearied faces,
Is a world all in reverse, left by
Skies' sympathetic tears.

On a pale, low-lit day of skeletal trees –
Black branch the fireworks,
Across a puddle's smooth white sky!

15

Against the lowering grey-black road,
Nestling less than forgotten,
Jagged ribbons glanced by light
Become a silver lining.

The barren moon, abandoned in the gutter:
A silver coin, a hope,
In a sea of galacial milk.

Cold's bitter touch and the care-full stamps
Of leaden feet, icebreakers,
Leave shattered-mirrors shimmer bright,
To crack self-disillusion.

Evening Walk

Months in the womb of breeding city lights,
And at last, freedom to trawl this countryside
Seems hazily pointless to unwary limbs.
Suddenly the twilight-troubled green
Swirls around swound-dark;
Sweeps me into a Rackham-coloured wood -
All lilac-fawn in the autumn moon's solstice;
And passing pools of quiet reflectiveness
I fly into the sky I sail by.

Now, downing the richest russet course
Of foliage: sinking silkly through a pelt
Of shadowy, lilting, fur-amber, racing -
Valleys wait, verdantly hovering
To catch me in hollows;
Swing, with marine gentleness, around;
With gracious 'suasion tempt yet one dance more;
Where longing avenues of sylvan limbs
Stretch solemnly and arch in harmony.

The feathered darkness there is purple-warm,
Staccato-edged with chuttering birds' last song:
Embrace of muffling magic bestilling -
Thronging breaths of shadows' beating hearts
Float in suspension;
Clinging – till the darkness must begin
And wake to living, hunting, fleet searching –
To tremulous harmony of the hour
Beguiling the lithe souls of everything.

The Field

The green, a subtle green
that would not jump to meet you,
but intertwined its grassy shades
softly within your eyes,
lay like a tranquil sea beneath the sky.

In the corner of vision
the sun stood, brilliantly
pure white, like light of innocence,
and its aureole
sprayed shimmering silver through the ark of dawn.

It scattered diamonds down
on the waves in exuberance,
sparkling, washed infinitely
reflected, glorified,
dancing a dance too fine for human eyes.

In the midst, were we
welcomed - nor knowing why -
into a sanctum; poised in
a mystery, floating:
the waves of lightness washed into our souls.

· · ·

Once more we walked there.

The sun which had then stood,
with splendid dignity,
had gone - hidden, its passage now,
veiled by dim clouds,
waiting, in hazy, dark solemnity.

18

A shadow had fallen,
and complex currents flowed
between us – new tension rippled:
dividing, and binding.
But sighed the soft, skeletal-bearing air,

though tangs of decay keened,
and something melancholy
knew of our subtle strife – whispered
a hint, in troubled breath:
Infinitesimal perfection there -

Latent, nascent in things:
the once perlucent vision;
even the splintering, jaded gulfs
washing our feet – gleamed hope,
reflecting rays of light hidden above.

Reaction

At last! I too could will to *want* to splutter forth
loathing of Nature's ugfulness; struck by
this stench-shot rot-black swathe
of once-water....now a congealed disc
where pitch past pitch of murk
suggests despair's side of a coin.

Low squat toads can't abide its wallowing inertia;
only mosquitoes flit de-lighted, stir
the flaccid gel to shiver;
my stomach churned, I fall head-
long to rest my blackened brow
upon a chastened tree.

Solidly writhe up, slower than time, petrified
monsters: branches fallen of a fruitless tree, succumbed
to buried vigilance,
vengeful looking; stirless air stagnates
that eye and fearful are
the thoughts that creep therein.

One great dark eye of malice, that pool burns
into the mind that sees it with a curse;
staring from earthy ground;
swallowing light.... When suddenly I see:
its blackest point reflects
the sky's fine architects:

Slim trees, fingers, brushing with soft design,
trace meaning in a morsel of glass-air
trapped in this monstrous gaze.
A gleam relief, of beauteous normalcy -
a window in a cell
to draw the soul from hell.

Lifted! - a timorous child my soul - shamefaced
at ever doubting Nature's mothering glance,
whose birth-bond is a pact:
For when I fall, her wild, subtle glee
distracts my saddened heart –
and I defend her part.

Many a time, when suffering's stroke has pierced
through tender spots of feelings sensitive,
have I wandered to her:
To be bewitched, with lovely promise there,
and all her moods I know -
her light; her deathly snow.

Never has she been absent when I sought;
revealing nothing of her secrets; grudged
some solace at her worst;
No more shall I betray her varied form -
Mother's splashed purity -
with dark antipathy.

Faux Pas

Wandering in a foreign by-way,
my head wreathed in dreams of anglogenic form -
all my senses keenly stirring
with the thirst for nature's nourishing repast
of beauty; Suddenly raised a chill;
conscious of inherent estrangement:
my guilty mind's tongue.

Syllable's utterance merely,
can betray unsympathetic person's mind
of patriotic 'notusness'
to the censoring ears of fellow humankind.
And nature? Are myriadic sprites
prickling now - incongruity felt
in my native muse?

Is the sibilant stream hissing?
Are the leaves a-tremble at *my* treading there?
Do their animae resent me?
Do the bulls see scarlet as I wander past?
No matter. I'll dream in my own words -
thread thoughts of white and crimson
through the lanes of France.

Ripening

Why *fill all fruit with ripeness to the core?*[1]
Maturing fruit is bitterest by the skin!
Rich sun, bright rain, expansive air galore,
But slowly, from the heart, sweet softness win;
The secret centre, stirring at the breath
Of nature, drinks, transforms the loving rays,
Within itself; beauty returns the gaze.
The Earth's an open book: of life and death,
That exiled man may read, be touched, and learn;
Parables stand in solid stone, fires burn
With passion's tale, lore in the serpent's twined;
So men - fruit of one tree, and all a-kin -,
Grow silently, from heart and soul and mind:
Bright bloom without, goodness stems from within.

---

[1]   Keats' 'Ode to Autumn'.

Gnats

Gnats dancing: choice, but rarely watched:
                            a weaving, wonderous sight!
Above the silver river, but a shade beyond the sward:
A gentle throng float leisurely as
                            leaves the waves of wind;
Arrowlike others pierce the milling cloud in arcing flight.
A moment: breeze scattered husks drift;
                            the next, with swift accord
In lilting concert sweeps, with courteous
                            swirl, one flying form;
Or blows intense a twirl of spiral sparks: a fountain light.
While noble men's perfect designs
                            are shattered by discord,
These strange, infernal, ghostly pests
                            dance in sweet harmony.
Torturing sprites, they're no more pricked
                            by our rage's vent,
Than laughing Fortune gilding Dante's
                            heaven with merriment.

The Wind

Why, why do you wound me so, Wind?
Heal my heart to break?
You sing the skies,
Laugh sober earth to scorn.
There dancing with the flowers,
Before my eyes?
Whispering through the trees
Your lovely lies.

Whither will you carry me, Wind?
When, when will it be?
Water leaps high,
The Light with you flies past;
Since dawn your voice was calling,
A yearning sigh,
A whoop of promised pleasures -
Here am I.

Where, where are the dreams you brought?
There, hovering high!
Ephemeral scenes,
As vivid as the day;
Stir limbs as flow the thoughts there,
Seeking joy's streams;
Your palace formed from fine air,
Falls to dreams.

Whence whirl you so hastily, Wind?
Where, where do you fly?
The light leaves prance,
Die in mad ecstasy.
Sudden unseen caresses;
a wild sweet dance;
soon sighing last embraces;
fading romance.

First Thaw

The grass crouches bedraggledly
Tawny and green, and vulnerable;
Shyly the teardrop dew a-gleam,
Softly breathing, salt-tinged air -
Till the wind tosses fir branches,
Like a girl impulsive
Tossing back her hair.

Evaporating snow splendours,
Gently glowing, perspiring:
A lady's powdered, sparkling, skin,
When melody and movement's ceased,
Heart yet dancing in the wavelets
Of the wake of music,
Poise pale and serene.

As though the world, in winter deep -
A debutante, a princess chaste -
Were raptured in a midnight dream:
An aerie sapphire fantasy,
Where the dancers whirled like snowflakes,
In palatial splendour,
Velvet, crystal, ice;

Reality came dawning down,
Raining a shower of shivering life,
Of sober thought and wakeful hope:
A tender youthful agony;
Till the twilight spell aspiring,
Her cheeks flush softly,
Eyes fill with blue dreams.

A Window on the Night

As the evening closes,
Shepherds in the deeds of day,
To shelter in the sure folds of the mind;
Sprightlier memories gambolling through the night,
The rest, appointed time now passed,
Settling to slumber for eternity;
Darkness awakens
Nocturnal cares and tasks:
Thronging swarms of duties left behind;
Ghosts of worries shallying from the light,
Roaming, tracing well-worn paths,
Ever unseeing, watching me.

Then a window opens,
Like a mirrored sorcery,
Realms vivid, yet always beyond reach:
Spell-binding pictures gaze and magnetize,
Enamelled tinctures shine and laugh,
Oil-rich landscapes lure like wine.
These are the counties
Of Night-Viewed-Distantly;
Body propped or curled in casement niche,
Light spirit, swallow-like, flees to those skies:
Monumental fantasies,
Ebon-dark midnight sunshine.

There live salamanders
Like liquid leaves of fire
In jetty pools; there riots the parade:
Blazing flares, to elven revels borne;
Whirl, lunaphile dervish bats,
Where effluates th'albescent stream.
In the darkest regions
Are clustered burning jewels:

Luminant but when the light doth fade.
Comely deeps frail glimmerings adorn,
Pinnate velvets, gossamers,
Waft and wreathe through Night's demesne.

A demitinted etching
In winter breathes a sigh:
The muted melody of time.
Eloquent elegance and old-world charm:
Trees and shadows shyly talk;
Ice arrays its glyptic lace.
In the hush of snow-light
A caution and a call,
Chilling, tempting beauty in the rime.
Silvispheric cadences disarm
Where the waiting fair-folk stage
Magic trial of grudge or grace.

Wearily I cast me
Into the whelming sky:
Empyrean pool of ever-haling blue.
Stars print light upon my searching soul
Images of sparkling joy,
Ciphers of a tender word.
Yet when I turn homeward
Into my self again,
Though I sped my spirit as it flew,
Nought recounts it of its distant goal:
Stirring as in infant sleep,
Murmurs memories unheard.

Ablation

A woman weeps in ice.
And none can ease or staunch her tears,
for she is set apart.
Blue as the distant years -
where once she foamed with laughter,
gilded ocean of the south -
White, near translucent, ghostly;
but the straining of her mouth,
her tears, speak her humanity:
the struggle to repress,
mute battles raging in the heart.

We do not know her name;
though many seek to own her fears
and advertise their cause.
There is no-one who hears
the unseen thoughts that thunder
behind indigo eyes,
closed to our looks of sympathy,
our questions and our lies.
Alone, between the rocks, the sea,
she offers her witness
for all and so in anguish thaws.

Musing on Trees

How does a tree decide which way to grow?
Does it ponder each tendril in silent retreat:
Blooms of wisdom the knarled kindly trunks seem to
                                                show,
Every turn a new stroke, the design to complete?
Or do buds of desire explode from the grass,
Each inch tingling potentially, springing with sap?
So impulsive the moments of miracle pass
As new tendrils reach airily, chosen by hap?

Perhaps a tree lolls through a long life of leisure
Deliciously stretching at will to the sky?
Laughing at humans all rushing for pleasure,
Who, whilst they are rising, grow old, sicken, die.
Yet somehow in earnest they seem to ascend,
Though their million light little hands are awave
To all passers by, and though their heads gently bend,
There is pride in their stance and their venture is brave.

Are they falling through air slowly like liquid dream,
Quite amazed at the visions weird winding below?
Their branches and leaves floating hair in the stream
Of a wonderland, where restless, rootless things grow!
Or kinetic vitality, burning in sight:
Solemnities' fireworks, illumining rays
Soar and spread and etincillate through the vault's night,
Spelling beauty on mystery, arboreal phrase.

Before the Storm

A herald of dark light, a premonition
Of glory and of violence on the wing,
Rousing the spirit's awe and shaking from it
Sunny-day complacencies which cling.

As arrows in time's warping grasp,
sunbeams occluded glide,
Blazoning the ultimatum
of the glowering vault;
Swiftly commandeering earth's soft
feathers as they fly,
Burnishing the woodpidgeon
with lustre of the armoured sky.

Below, the fawn fur smoulders, roads
and rocks are turned to iron,
The dusty grass is gilded and the
air is soft as tears;
A silent transformation: earth is
robed in solemn sheen -
Only a bit of bitter blue hovers,
holds truce, between.

Now cloud and land is mingled,
and verdant is the heaven,
While light like love or hate a golden
web between them weaves.
Surrounded by the darkness,
colour bristles to relief;
Is such precious prophecy
worth all the looming grief?

No rainbow could bestow like irri-
descence on the world,
Or make the eye so dance with joy
and nerves like blossoms spring.
The mantle of the storm is trimmed
with re-creation's fire;
Slumbering voices find new tongues
to charm the dragon's ire.

The brooding thunderhead and radiant vision:
Both symbol and key of the unknown.
So awakened instinct thrills a pondering mind,
Beneath a firmament of abalone.

La Petite Maine

Gushing down the weir, unwearied wave
Flings the quaint old mill a sparkling glance;
Hushing noise whirls round the sounding spell:
A glassy plain is spun like sorcery
To creamy lava, seething ivory.

Brighter than the foam, across the strait,
Gold, green, blazons sweep the falling time;
Lacery of crosses, veil immaculate,
Adorns for brides the convent's final bed.
Trees of shadow sorrow overhead.

*

Silent mirror pools, so calmly clear,
Repeat a dream-blue heaven of liquid air;
Mosaic of floating catkin's stippled curls
Frames the lofty poplars' airy grace,
Garnet strands and amber twine embrace.

Casting off finesse of borrowed plumes,
Solemnly the river world reflects;
Inward looks, where creeping creatures grow;
Water powdered with applish tinted bloom
Throws galaxies about its native gloom.

Downstream spreads the verdant wing of death:
Stifling quilt of vivifying green;
Lonely, meditative rippling depths
Breathe in concert with the quiet sky;
Precious draughts the drowning realm supply.

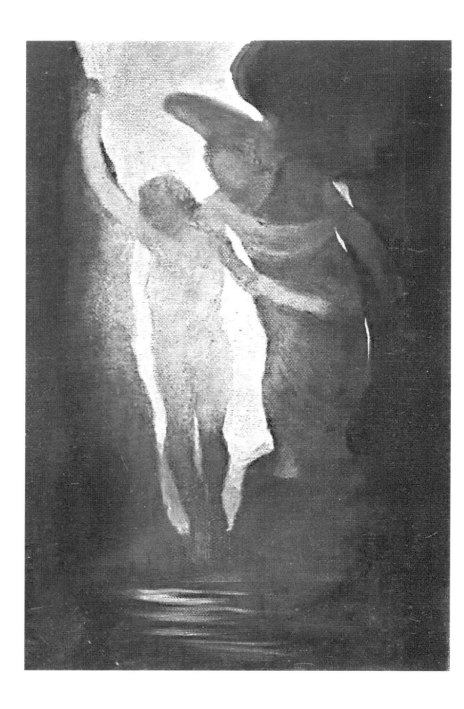

36

Time and Change

Keys

In the days when our street was two kingdoms -
"Up the Street" and "Down the Road",
with our house between,
and trees towered near to the sky -
a large lady shuffled, and shuffled,
always going by.

She is sentinel, fraught with her duty,
though weary and sore with long days;
her thoughts and her back
bent on something nobody else sees;
and dancing in rhythm behind
are her jingling keys.

Her slippers heel-worn, and her cardi
shapeless, as though it were stuffed
with mind-sparks she feeds
upon, souvenirs shifting like sands
as she shuffles, chewing the keys
in ruminant hands.

She would sway in her pacing to greet us
smiling a watery blue,
an indistinct word;
But when her grown son caught her eyes -
her own reflected: four windows
on bright Polish skies.

While his strength stood there she straightened,
gazing on dreams in the flesh -
a key to the past,
treasure of the future, and voice:
for him she stood and she talked
of her life and her choice.

I do not know what she spoke of,
only that privations were joys,
a gift to her child;
where her cottage stood, there was a shrine,
and her love of the past and the future
has passed into mine.

Candle Lady

My granny is like a candle -
So the doctor says –
She's melting away; and I can see
she's white and as time goes by
becomes more droopy,
and decorative too.

She sits there in the evenings
with a halo shining round her head
and tints the world with
an atmosphere of mystery,
secrets, adventure;
brings to life the ancient times.

Her laugh like a guttering flame
makes the walls themselves
jump with excitement.
She throws soft light on obscure things;
is a heart of warmth
which draws all wanderers in.

I want to shield her brightness
from harsh winds,
from all effects of time,
but must not stop her shining.
When a time unthinkable comes
and with her darkness falls:

Against its black her memory
will be some light; Like wax
as she melts she spreads,
and sticks in fantastic
pools of ideas; inspired dreams burn
kindled by her love.

Time and Place

...But nowhere seems to me to ebb
The air of history's reverence
More than a pocket clump of trees,
Set in a childhood field.

The meteor which perhaps fell
And struck that hollow in the hill,
Has burned through time and flamed across
My sight – richly to fertilize
That island of green trees;
Sowing Imagination's seed,
Casting the day-dreams' thrall.

The dead flames of a shooting star,
Sere catapult, kindled our play;
Ardent the battles fought within
Its mouldering, blood-spiced dip.
Converging valleys caught the eye
In tactical quandary, planning war.
The charge its slopes still bear pulses
With standards' fluttering call.

Or in its depth we weathered months
Swallowed by a big-bellied ship.
A band of wild hearts pent within,
Without the wildness tossed;
Dark air-brushed leaves above at once
Were the mottled sky-of-the-storm,
And the slishing sound of the sea surging
In stirring currents round.

We struggled against witchery's
Insidious creep up on the soul
Out-casting evil's urge in fear
With prayers or blinding blame.
And vivid as remembered days
True-hearted characters of myth
With whom I wondered as we sought
Adventure's holy grail.

Adolescent

I'm a neanic, manic entropy –
Intrepid: In whorled ecstasy
And bitter heart-pangs
Twisted, screwing through the world:
I'll emerge noumenously,
In clear self-lit bliss,
Or die like this.

Crush[2]

It's just a little crush.
I flame, grow faint,
Dreaming of your touch.
It's just some trivial fling
Of my emotions, hormones,
Changing everything.

It's not that everything I do
Revolves around you.
Just that my breath is drawn by you;
Each deed once done,
Beyond control,
Spins off before your eyes –

If you were watching.

---

[2] The first lines of this poem were suggested by and are hence indebted to the song 'Crush' by Jennifer Paige.

And the form of you
Is the tension that pulls
Through me like a puppet's strings,
Keeping me buoyant.
And the force of you
Is the magnet of my thoughts,
And the stifling of my dreams.

Epiphany?

I walk along the road with my hands in my pockets.
Like a figure of Nemesis, long-black-coated
beneath grey-faced sky, a self-effacing witness.
The trees weep over me, walls are rising, soft but stern,
to close my sense of freedom to a letting go,
happy vapidity in the wind that's flown away.
I look down, only a stubborn chin holding out
against my own mean, hollow, hunched shrivelling –
And leap into my eyes, my heart, my soul!
through glum-gauzed veils of apathy, the
living, glowing colours of slight, lost leaves.
Abandoned innocent treasures. They soak
into my mind. On sudden impulse -
(for no-one is around) - with abandon
I gather them, scrabbling in the dirt, to
fill my pockets; fill myself with beauty
'till again I rise. And stalk blackly down the road.
Realise that my pockets have holes in them made by
my gnawing fingers, and the leaves are trapped forever,
far within my dark defence. But my cloak is all
spilt-littered-silk-leaf-lined with the colours of sun-blood.
In my thoughts I go; heart beating to know
a hidden joy inside.

44

People of the Street

There was a man I would avoid,
barrelling down the street.
Large and inconvenient,
a stomach (I presumed) and head
of great proportions (so he said)
abroad on two left feet.

From his mouth would roll the words,
rounded, and hit the ground,
like finely crafted marbles:
polished, pretty, useless craze,
and as I went a rattling phrase
behind me still would bound.

All too often he would lurk,
en route to the station;
grey and khaki, grease and dust,
his city-slob apparel topped
by intellectual glasses stopped
our tracks in consternation.

Mr Pomposity we called him
in his bubbling pride;
Juggernauting with his noise
a humble man's impatience, we
would rationally assume that he
must be the same inside.

There is a woman now I know
lives by her garden gate.
Ready with a hailing cry
she draws you on a wordy thread
and spins it swiftly round your head
 - you cannot help but wait.

She'll prod you with her questions,
repeating every theme;
and much too loud for comfort,
you'll hear your comment, smile or frown
broadcast blithely to the town
along with her next scheme.

She has her own opinions -
very much her own -
At certain local subjects,
I find I have to turn my head
to hide the fact my cheeks are red
or leave her quite alone.

Just recently we touched upon
her family history.
I will not here report the tale;
suffice to say, complacence shook,
and I cannot forget the look
of stale misery.

And so when we are shopping,
I do not dodge her aisle,
or linger when out walking
because she's dawdling ahead -
I charge on up the hill instead
and give her my best smile.

A Change

My life becomes a nursery rhyme,
My thoughts are an infant's song.
As strange, as simple, danced by time,
As sad, as sweet, so long.

I move to a tune that I've known since the womb,
It has slept in my own all these years.
It's as sweet and as slow,
As the waters which flow,
At summer's dawn, over the weirs.

Yet now we embark on a marvellous quest
And adventure pursues us apace;
With a child at the helm,
Through a nebulous realm –
With no torch but the beams from his face.

Infant's reaction to a doll

A cold thing that makes as if to live!
A pretty thing, with limbs livid and stiff.
A child, with eyes frozen,
who sits on mummy's knee,
with horrid stillness takes the place of me!

A friendly thing who waves in mummy's hand?
Small awkward person - do you understand?
Poor bundled helpless body,
baby with rubber skin,
Get off mummy's lap and let me in!

Dolly lying crooked on the floor,
will you move if I approach some more?
Will you let me take you
into my arms and power?
Use you as my baby for an hour?

You are mine now, strange, humanish thing:
for me you'll dance or cry, for you I'll sing.
And I'll give you my thoughts,
since you belong to me.
Approaching stranger - Do not touch my baby.

Bratz

Pretty Karly, five, is sitting,
gazing at her latest doll.
What allure! Her eyes are shining,
lips are pouting, always posing
with sweet nonchalance the envy
of a gangster's moll.
This doll wears the edge of fashion,
clothes like in the magazine.
Clothes to show the limbs that wear them
- maybe Karly's could be like them
if she only raised her seam?
Little Karly practices *that look*
before the glass at home:
Arms akimbo, shoulders sassy,
hips aswaying, final touch
with Mum's mascara comb.

Baby Karly goes to meet the
world, in custody of Dad;
Dressed up in the clothes he bought her
like the pretty Bratz dolls wear;
lipstick too - she feels great, why
does her Gran look sad?

Clever Karly talks the talk now
and has nearly got the strut;
All she needs are three-inch heels
- but her parents just won't buy them.
They're stuck in a rut.
Karly's friends think she's the coolest
yet *their* parents buy them shoes.
What use are a family
if, when they are buying presents,
you don't get to choose?

Friendly Bob, thirty, is sitting,
gazing at that little girl....

49

Chorleywood "Lawn Cemetery"[3]

Little clumps of flowers
carefully, memorially placed
in the faultless sheet
of ever-living green;
But with no tombstones,
no nameplates recording memory's ….
Could it really be a *lawn* cemetery?
People have gravestones,
and the pets whose owners want
to give them a "proper burial";
Even animals have names.
But the green, green grass….
where you reclined, I close beside,
drunk on a wish fulfilled
dreamt life together..
Which, vivid like an emerald,
is held precious not for what it's worth
but for sentimental value.
Whose sharp blades
shivered the pronouncements of relatives
with youth's delusions
as they fell to earth.
Sliced them into needle-pricks
to nag forever,
smashed embarrassed shards,
or bouncing bangers of
laughter repressed till explosion point.
Lawns are therapeutic patches,
Nature's healing-in-a-pocket,

---

[3]   I passed this place near my grandmother's and did not see any
tombstones - I suppose there must be plates of some sort recording the dead
who lie there, but the initial impression puzzled my imagination with this quirky
result.

50

or men's seedling dreams
of acres to be earned.
Softest sunbeds, sulkers' solace,
what a multitude of secrets
they could tell! And
what monstrosities lurk in
their junglous depths for
children's eyes.
Lawns have a life.
From green innocency
they go through sloughs
of muddy despondence,
to rich fertile impingeingness.
And sympathetic piteous days,
when the heat of life
has dried them out,
they dress sadly in khaki.
A lawn, a friend, is always there,
a silent witness, recipient
of scenes to shame all fiction's
tales. A stage on which we
play some part, until life's
act is done; a modest
source of sweet refreshment;
and a tactful veiler of our
faults at last.
Wouldn't you give your lawn a grave?

In Denial

We forget the use of shoulders:
Cliffs of beauty starkly sweep,
draw eyes to depths and vaults;
Sole supports of ancient world,
Atlas showed how constant strength
must repair our faults.
Still, the lodge of human power
in lands where people toil,
bearing burdens of their kin
and fructifying soil;
Where we lift our pride to gleam,
there our exaltation raised esteem.

We scorn the support of knees:
Angles merciful await
soul or body as it falls -
save them from a heavier hurt,
plead for grace, the final hope -
where the rest appalls.
Now they are too fine, too stiff
to reverence the Most High;
with them harden selfish hearts,
closed to laugh or sigh.
Thrones where children rule above;
 seat of dear possessions, seat of love.

We will not fulfill breasts:
Tender vessels brim and pour,
nourish body and soul;
mouths and hearts drink elixir:
vigour, comfort, trust -
she who gives, made whole.
Glory of a woman's form,

52

the sweeter if their own!
Softest pillow for a head,
refuge, if theirs alone.
Trafficked treasure on display,
though their finest use is hid away!

We butcher the fruit of our womb:
Inner sanctuary where one,
devoted, entered in;
where the gift divine, of life,
all potential, could become
future promise, from joy been.
What was once the safest home -
become a slaughterhouse;
private sphere of woman's care -
political warehouse.
The greedy hire; the barren starve or steal,
the blessed wound themselves and cannot heal.

*

We refute the dimension of Time:
Vantage point over the past
we fear heights where we stand;
history has taught us this -
the privilege inheritance
heaps burden with command.
Deny the wisdom age confers
or fall upon our knees;
Stifle breath of ripening years,
for death is a disease!
So we build our work to fall,
silence the alarm of history's call.

Anthem of the Twentieth Century

Inert the blocks, the towers our people raise;
No stone shall grow, untamed, beneath our hand.
All bright the beams which highlight our great land;
No mystery shall elude through shimmering haze.
No secret lives, we shall not understand,
Technology shall show and tell us all:
Dissect the past, create what shall befall,
Over the Universe, give Us command.
For we shall master time and space and thought,
And order life and health and happiness;
No voice shall speak to us out of distress -
We need no truths which are so dearly bought.
So we dictate, until our final breath;
One word remains unspoken - that of Death.

To an Infant

Look at me.
Let me whisper to your soul
Through the window;
While only sunlight
Bars, only promise
Fills, only trust
Asks.

Welcoming wells:
I shall pour within my
Being, words and feelings;
Too soon the sheen of
Glass, the veiling
Lace, the velvet
Swathe.

Flower-like, I leave
Promise which will wither:
Perfect beauty:
A true ideal of
Love - unstinting,
Immaculate and
Wise.

Hushed, I peer, at
Sanctuary within;
Before the portals close and
Sacred drama shall begin:
The resolution of a
Destiny. And we who
Touch you,
Move the scenes in place -

See not the crucial drama
Vivid with eternal grace.

The time will come:
Each curtain shall fall; all
Eyes will meet;
With only Light to
Spill, only Truth
Reply, and all
Fulfilled.

58

Love and Friendship

To a Friend

My friend, whose pure goodness of heart
gets babbled in sound-bites;
whose love shines from your mouth, in warmth of tone
so sweet that, though we are alone,
I crinkle with embarrassment inside:
thinking your gentleness uncouth,
wronging your "good-old" rightness,
cavilling at verbal caresses,
incredulous of such open truth -

Now, bitter though it was to down
conviction's ignorance,
in candied phrases, fashioned, honeyed, made
(as cutting-edge), your own; pained
though I was, your *gesture* made me feel,
understand the mild soul's generous power.
Warm fuzzy feeling? Nonsense!
It's the glow of stirred, breathing, embers,
or a glimpse to the heart of a half-furled flower.

Rebecca's Ring

Some things capture a person;
Things, gestures. It caught my eye
every time she shook her hand –
Not loose-wristed flicks careless,
but determined like shaking a pepper-pot. As though
jerking the meaning
out of her words
for all to SEE.
Shaking by gesture
other people's minds
to make them MEAN.

On her finger: that ring caught her.
Bolder than convention,
sterling-hearted sun-flower blue.
Irreverently happy. Melancholically true.
Flaunted, bloomed on her finger
a rare fruit of motherly love;
rebellious seal received by
a wild questioner of form:
Informal floral, tears collected,
shaped to keep the eyes' smiles warm.
Embraced her finger in a
unique glimpse of hidden truth –
Captivating.

Prodigal (a farmer's son)

Broken loose -
Aye; I've snapped
The sapling roots which bound,
For boundlessness
Of land, of wave, of sky;
To flit the heavy sod
Torn my own heart.
Shaking the shackles off
My dancing, wandering feet -
I shook the dust,
Half-witting, in your eye,
To blind you to this face
Which listened long.

Tried, I, to be patient;
Your patience never tried
In telling me,
Imparting Law and land.
For fondness I stood close
And seemed to see.
Those hours, solid as oak,
Father, as true English,
Slow love grew strong –
Till brave to take command,
In honour of your strength,
I would be gone.

I have wandered freely
At will – and I am proud
That my soul was
Not buried in the ground:
A life of rooted growth
Seems death to me.

Yet in solitude's dream
Swung moments on a peak
Or in a trough
Of dusk; I fear the sound
Of bells ringing far faint
In memory.

I find myself, grasping
In absent mindfulness
A rasping stem,
A reassuring staff,
As though it were a trowel;
To toss back time.
Running my fingers o'er,
Familiar textured thoughts
Press round me.
I hitch my breath and laugh,
And climb a hill to see
What's next to see.

But yet my heart hearks back
For voices from the past.
Light shoulders miss
The heavy hand thrown off;
Eyes dwelling on new con-
tours see lost smiles.
And I would gladly take,
Unflinching at the grain,
Servitude's spade
Upon my back: a cross
Bourne right around the world,
To wake dead love.

Hidden Depths

Once, sudden betrayal
By a face that spoke no guile:
Always a fearful, cliff-edge lure,
To pry away each painted mask
Of human flesh
And see the twisting wile.

A dark disturbing dream
But strengthened in denial;
Until the day I tore upon
A tender, germinating truth,
A growing grace -
And found it was fragile.

And now my spirit yearns
To break but one more seal,
For hid in you I hope to find
The greatest treasure of the mind:
Honesty
Which has the power to heal.

66

Angel

Below a sheltering arc of chiselled wing,
held in sweet curves of sculptured smile:
jewel memories of this *dear one*,
treasure of many hearts.
Reliquary of love incorrupt;
silent paragon of intercession.

Compassionate guard of the grave -
How stiff and solid, cold I seem,
pent within a hidebound heart
from sympathy outpoured;
watch this mortal grief - who will not turn,
seeing in my form no consolation.

Oh granite angel, I too sob:
for those who watch the cold interred;
for what is buried in my heart;
to be a comfort here.
Stone is granted sacramental grace
longing cannot write upon my face.

Show

You look upon me kindly:
a fiber-optic twinkle
glancing down pathways of nerve.
Distracting impulse -
a show of light to please
kept in reserve.

A pretty thing displayed here;
scintillating fibrils
wake a quizzical delight.
Display of tinsel -
an artificial tree,
morbidly bright.

Why such a pageant,
when I to you am little
and our friends are nearly all?
A guilty quittance,
or genuine, this bounty
to the small?

I try to look within you
to see the images
you cherish there;
Mirrors defeat me;
Turn on a smile to dazzle
and beware.

Innocent?

There's no resentment clear in your eyes now;
too subtle-sunk beyond the reach
of words skimming to fish it
from those pools.

A moment of pure openness there seen
lets all of my unease well in
beneath it's gleam, *because*
all seems right.

Your smile captivates, slender arms coax
mischief, or simple happiness;
Strands of your will caress then
tight entwine.

A subtle grasp of loving treachery:
storms rive and darken silken cool,
stir flying fears, raptorous hate -
and sorrow.

And then incomprehension sweetly may
be calm's redawn, or guilt's veneer
upon your gaze; and bitter
its salt-twinkle.

Moments were enough, peaces of joy,
communing in a halcyon spell,
that I should wait beside you
with my dreams.

The promise of adventure beckons there;
the depths to sound; the tranquil beach
where all forgetful laughs
a child's delight.

I long to stay the still tempestuous powers
from devastation, build on beauty rare,
turn wilderness to Eden
sweet and wild.

But never shall I find the treasure lost
I seek, the miracle of love
and trust unbridled: perfect
Innocence.

Untitled

She is not here,
the woman you desire;
raising your torch of chaste
and guarded fire.

By your request
alone, I take her place;
if once I see and trust
your shadowed face.

Your tales of distant lands
are colourful, and just;
rousing intrigue in you
like wanderlust.

70

Your gifts are deep-sea pearls,
exquisite and rare;
each in another's life
buys you a share.

Your arguments are waves:
wonderous worthy reply -
'til heedless of my stance,
they surge on by.

With proud delight I see
your admiration's charm;
yet fear enchantment's tower
brings us harm.

For I am no ideal
that courtly deeds may win -
my fall would gouge your eyes
on thorns of sin.

Though I would go with you,
I will not be a sham -
Remove the veil and see me
as I am.

Baptism by Fire

Sitting in the dim morning,
waiting. Heart-pulse suspended
in a hollow, barely there
as tip-of-the-tongue drops of
mist in the rough-gem air.

Your advent, silent, condenses
liquid the light of sun-beads
into fire through each limb.
I don't see you, I feel you;
I am a flame within.

Transparent, innocent, naïve,
as dew, freshly dropped down here,
I have swum, drunk on clear life,
As free as the fog, as cool,
as calm. Now tenses strife.

Clarity reflects myriad
shapes, arabesques flame, dance;
reflections, glam'ring my veins
to flush in enchantment,
with colours or with stains?

Breaks, glorious confusion
– sun's translucent pearl smashed
on Eve's rock, grey with wives' tales —
sparks through my fresh vision;
a new life unveils.

Your Eyes

There's a sunflower blown in your eyes:
The intensest of blossoming joys;
Tender reflection of flames bright above
In the murk-sheen of
Dove-blue-grey skies.

They widen and deepen and yawn –
Sweeping vault turns to vault in the heart
Where the liquid veins seeping from volcanic depths
Glow with passionate heat,
Fire unborn.

Yet the coolest of new moons, crescent,
Lies pearl-gleaming in a stirred pool
When the light strikes soft waters, where waving branches
Through caerulous shallows
Are bent.

The arc of a deep woodland dell
Is my refuge – the peace in your eyes
Is in golden-lit verdure of glades where I dream –
And find sunflower joys beam
Their spell.

Testimonial

My love is as harsh as a savage bramble, clinging
To offer fruitfulness sharp-sweet;
                    sun distilled through earth's tears.
Gentle my man, as a raven's feather floating
On the breeze; of knightly time's compassion,
                          soft dark secrets' pall.
My lord's as solid as a mountain you'd build hopes upon-
Unmoving thane of thunderous clouds,
                        whose fury flashes fierce.
My friend's eyes shine with the
                    mysterious warmth of candles,
Liquidly alight in pools of shadows
                      dancing with my dreams.

Apologia

You called me; a swan, dark swan, your swan.
My heart calls you, my hirondelle:
Herald of light, warmth, new life to me!
Its sounds curve silkly, swirl within,
Sharp, solonelle and beautiful.

You see a swan. My waiting there,
For you is poetic significance, white joy
Upon the lake of dusk and dragonfire.
But I am mute; while you happily praise –
Singing, outpouring your soul-full.

74

I, musing, long; that you should know
My silent glide about your path
Describes more love all-lost-for-words
Than dreams could draw. And if some fate
Should blast a tragic end to all
Then you should be my swan-song.

Love Song

Your kisses fall upon me like raining star-flowers,
Fragmenting my thoughts with blessings;
And I become a river of rejoicing,
Leaping dissolved with joy – laughing
To catch your lightening love-fall;
Flowing from the Source of glory
To deep seas' embrace.

My love for you wells in waves of tranquil tumult,
Swinging through my steps and vision.
And you abide in joyous ever-moving-
ness the world I sail upon – or dive
Into to bathe in wonder;
As a sea of glass like crystal
Winking at the stars.

The morning stars sang when we shall make our love known.
Their echoes ripple in your figure now.
And we shall dance like saplings in the blowing
Breaths of God's creation – swept
By Providential winds
Bringing fruitfulness with blessings
Showering from heaven

75

Betrayal

Do you remember, oh my daughter?
How joyously I ran down
to the lively river, to raise you up
whence you were playing
in the good, clean mud?
Your countenance was of love betrayed.
Breaking promises in your wideling eyes.

Your littleness was haunting, but the river,
frightening me with its power,
swept on regardless of man's control.
No living willfull
could arrest its course.
Your countenance was of love betrayed
Breaking promises in your wideling eyes.

I reached for support, as I held you;
knowing love's ties once there.
Grasped only air, sterile and cool.
And panic rocked me,
And my own grip loosed.
Your countenance was of love betrayed,
Breaking promises in your wideling eyes.

Could you forgive me, little daughter?
How easily love breaks down
at the kiss of Judas, the parting touch!
You were a memory
of a joining reft.
Your countenance was of love betrayed.
Breaking promises in your wideling eyes.

End of a Day

There's no tongue can tell of my heart's fall at morning,
There's no eye can weep as my soul ebbs at dusk.
For the stamens of lilies are gilded for silence,
My call flies unwitnessed,
Sunflowers turn their heads, shun my dark, as they must.

That beauty which senses my being's corruption,
Still stirs a pale breath with a longing for life.
That beautiful being betrayal has haunted,
Is my love past longing,
Is purity's pity in guise of a knife.

My mouth could not utter the words my mind painted
When, features remaining, my will turned to dust.
Yet the heat of that moment has hardened its image,
A cenotaph blackened,
Sphinx's mortal question which answer I must.

No song can call back the winged words I have uttered,
No tears can revive the dry soil in my heart.
For the dawn of the day sees the birth of the happy,
Sun's zenith bears witness;
The pallor of twilight is mourning our strife.

Womaniser

Behold vacuous empire in that man's eyes:
Magnetic void, dark depth which enthrals;
uncharted territory lures or appalls
the women he looks at -
a realm of incontinent skies.

See visions luciferous spark in those orbs:
Radiant energy leaps to devour
wondering satellites, fill them with power
of ideal and desire -
chimerical flames it absorbs.

Watch the rainbow of promises, glittering lies -
suns of hope beaming through aether of tears -
fade and relume as each new star careers
though enveloping clouds,
where permanent light cannot rise.

Turn from his gaze, yet feel it still burn!
Listen! through vapours of asteral gloom -
soft-sobbing tides of a deep-welling doom
floatingly surge
from darkness where memories churn.

Tribute
To my husband

Oh, he is the night! - The saving rite
Which stirs my soul to think;
His is the voice across the waves
Calling me from the brink;

A sail: a fragile, brave-flung wing
Glimpsed high on angry waves -
A sign of hope, a call to dare,
Challenging whilst it saves;

My spirit's very balance, equi-
Poise to my heart's flight,
That I may soar, elated -
Nor graceless then alight;

The warm embrace of dusk's own peace -
Garb of love's modesty -
With dreams illuminate,
Dark heaven of security;

The thunderous storm, breaking the cloud,
En-lightening, though it mourn -
Raining sweet patience through the dark,
Forge of a sparkling dawn;

He is the Spring, the quickening
Of love and life within -
Wakening to fresh Reality:
I shiver, and then sing.

Faith

Soul and Body

I too, have seen the Sacred Hour fly -
or felt her shadow fall as light wings lifted,
a glimpse of haloed feet which had passed by...
Her absence, in a breath held -
a crystal shrine to call her -
shattered by the preasure of a sigh.
What had I seen, in those shrouded moments?
Who was it spoke, in the silent dark
where all the world I knew was white
with noise - a deluge swept,
turbulent, round about
this ghostly Arc?
There was Immensity, into its bosom
I might have cast myself, had I known how -
and in its heart the question:
Love infinite asking vow for vow.
I paused...
Waiting for the perfect answer.
Found it not in my echoing brain
nor in the deepest rummage
of my shallow, cluttered heart;
so sought it with a plea -
the artless child's refrain,
expecting every answer from
the questioner again -
Self-searching did I from the Unknown part.

Beautiful was she, who hovered then and fled,
as though a living thread
in His angelic floating train.
Her features, through the billowing mystery
movingly veiled, yet spoke like friends to me:
childhood Saints each had some presence there;

In her embrace, a spirit's, I was drowned,
as air too rarified nascent soul to suffice;
she was, nor held, an attitude of prayer;
her eyes, most human, glowing charity…..
Then, the daily world impatient grew
into this porous mind, and she was gone,
without the slightest trace, and yet I knew
the purest part of all my soul, was she.

Never more that blessing has returned.
No more do I now wait for it, and long…
Whether she or I the other spurned,
God knows.
                    I would be urged
to think no longer of a failure past,
of the question none can answer and live on.
Cast off sad pretence of saintly strife,
yearning for a state forever gone.

Then shall I turn to my material self:
full blooded, sensual, carefree?
Play with her each day a double masque:
catching her mirrored wink
at the thoughts I dare to think;
smiling at the scarlet lips,
or the curve of breast and hips;
Absorbed in sheer sensation,
and the full preoccupation
of how to be somebody just like me?
What rich delights could I enjoy alone,
escaped from warning voice or duty's leash;
unblunted, shaded, by modesty's veil,
how brilliantly could I carve my niche!

But senses sate and starve over again;
and image is not person, as we find
once vicious attack of pinioned words
disembowels it, yet our heart lives on,
suffering, ashamed, for what is gone;
or in spirit, cancerous pride beguiles,
swells, smothers to death someone we knew,
while the bold persona struts and smiles.

No joy is simple in our daily life,
no element unblended in the earth.
A man unsouled echoes a hollow tree,
stark, sinister, stunted and doomed he;
So plucked flowers, gorgeous in decay,
in melting lines across the pavement stray:
women, from their conscience torn away.
My soul and body are one, and alive;
a marriage indissoluble, their faults,
but most, their selfish isolation halts
the flow of sweet and sorrow where they strive
to be a whole harmonious, and pray:
both only fulfilled when they both give:
I Am in both, and both for Him live.

Birthday

Lonely amongst a throng this birthday,
Hollowly hungering for joy,
Breaking free at last I wander -
Up the country lane, draw deep breath again,
Set thoughts free, cut these griefs asunder;
'Til small voices of the world, unseen,
Unheard before, wake my mind to wonder.

Sudden sweet zither from the hedgerows[4]
Trips my heart with subtle strings;
Harmonises with a harsher
Rusty low rocking: childhood's summer's swing -
 - A third voice serrated, sharp tanged: bitter
As a grass-green apple off the tree;
And a fourth, as bright and soft as silver.

Caressively the wind re-minds me,
'Till my heart in joy looks up:
With a sudden smile, yet tearful,
Sees the gifts arrayed, Love's beauty displayed:
Sun-gleam of dandelions, golden -
Ruby grapes, amethyst flowers -
Showering silver light from those dark clouds.

Down a woody path, the grasses
Graciously give their scented souls
When crushed; there small trees' low branches
Grope to embrace, sighing, full of grace
– Even brambles, clinging, knit thorns,

---

[4]   All the sounds here described are, in fact, some of the very different
voices of the insects which constantly sing in the hedgerows and fields of parts
of France, as long as the weather is warm.

Like the kindling grip of children;
To be gently, sweet-painfully disentangled.

All these signs of Time's affection;
All these tokens of new birth;
Bring to mind that prize - Perfection
Promised at the dawn, to each soul forlorn -
Ever whispered in the rushes,
Ever glimpsed in branches' span,
The promise of the God who was made Man.

The Abbey

The avenue lured, long and strange;
A gold light filtered through dark leaves
Of subtle guards: the arching trees
Enclosed the path to a new range
Of consciousness, it seemed to me:
A shadow-land of memory.

Flicks of light made twisted shapes -
Lost pieces of a jigsaw puzzle
Beneath my feet - the waking tunnel
Rustled as a throng of swishing capes:
The soft clothing of ghosts,
Stirring, watching at their posts.

Through a living, swinging, arch,
I walked; and in procession *they*,
Across the green grass, silent, fey,
Passed: a haunting, joyful march
Up to the Abbey, holding high
Her graceful summits to the sky.

Although the stones lay broken 'round
The temple waited, unforlorn:
The songs of praise had not all gone,
But, silent, swept the holy ground;
Still, the abbey's patient stance,
Robes her in a true romance.

I thought the ghostly mourners sang:
A chant around me seemed to fly
Upon the wind, the shadows' cry.
And as the echoes softly rang,
They seemed to ask me – Come November[5],
Far, far away – will you remember?

---

[5]   November - the month dedicated in Christian tradition, to remembering
the dead, beginning with the feast of All Souls, and immediately preceded by the
feast of All Saints.

Meditation Watching the Sea

My soul, my Lord, is like the sea:
A tide restless turns and tosses fluid depths;
Drawn by nature to reach a high,
Which searching proves but shallowness.
Bubbling over rocks and arid shells,
Dark pools which trap the substance of its being,
Leaving it a little lost,
Still it returns to break itself.

This tranquil green; Thy perfect peace,
Should be stained by no vice – yet here, witness,
– In clogging stretches – jealousy
Soaks my mind as oil the sea.

Translucent world: a vessel, womb,
Welled with the salt of life – should purely host
Myriad forms of graces lush –
Yet have I drunk pollution's gush.

The sighing sea is ever heaved
With longing gasps for Truth – its fury breaks
Wildly at Sorrow – yet I storm
At *my* small grief, and moan, forlorn.

A struggling cycle, being seems;
A-struggling – Sigh! call to my Being! Since
Only that exhalation, which is
Love and loss of life, may still
Soul's fluctuations here – dashing,
Tearing between stone 'altars'[6] and the depths:

---

[6] The 'altars' were a particularly deadly band of submerged rocks, named
thus for the number of their sailor victims, mentioned in the Aeneid, amongst
other places.

89

The heart from whence they took their form —
And bring me safely back to Thee.

Such terrible humility:
Soft and pure as remnant snow
                                on granite veined with lead,
Crossed by the blackening stamp of man's
                                unchanging deathward tread.
As starlight fallen light upon a
                                swallowing, miresome pool,
To decorate its loathsome glass and bring joy to the fool.

A man who sees through power's bars
                                the truth that all may see,
And though to man he owes this gift,
                                for Truth will not go free.
The glow of wonder and of pain
                                welled in innocents' eyes;
Submitting yet, with humble love,
                                to gods who will chastise.
The majesty of God's elect,
                                though stripped and shorn of pride;
In tranquil steps monarchs oppressed,
                                who for their children died.
The silence of the mother who is blessèd:
                                she who mourns;
The visage of the sacrificial lamb
                                pressed round by thorns.

Song to my Soul

Embattled soul – where have you fled?
And when will you return to me?
In truth, t'were better I were dead
Than that we had surrendered.

Together, through the longest years,
Of solitude, we strove our way;
Fighting the soft smiles and the tears
That stormed us from within.

My secret thought: no enemy
Could worst me more - because so close
Were you that I could never see,
Till too late, how I'd erred.

Always I loved you, sometimes loathed –
Selfish desire spurred me to drag
You from the One who had betrothed
Himself to you, through suffering.

Together we fought, one and one,
My loss always your victory.
This weird peace bids me fear I've won -
I wish my peace I'd tendered.

Embattled soul – where can I fly
To find you, to renew our life?
One chance remains – myself deny:
Christ may, my soul, salvation bring.

A Child

This child is the fruit of a hundred prayers,
Of a love all-giving, of a pain joy-bearing.
A bright shape of spirit, a soft form of flesh,
Now moulded by gestures, by glances and stares.

This child must still pass through a million tears:
Of his own heart's breaking, of his harsh will's making,
True born in the spirit, loving through the flesh,
May his soul grow in strength through his fears.

Dear Child, who, the fruit of all God's love given,
Offers love past knowing, from death new life flowing,
The gift of the Spirit alive in the flesh,
Bring our child in your likeness to heaven.

Rome

Oh, pines and fountains of Rome! and unwanted roses -
Abundance of flames in sharp gypsy hands -
Some thirst unquenchable seeps through clear fountains:
Insouciant, aching as children's demands.

Oh colours, fashions of Rome, and beautiful faces -
Cornucopia of smiles and lovely designs -
Some voice inaudible speaks - not perfection
But fear of joy's image the plaint in its lines.

Oh living ages of Rome, whose stones bear the graces,
Whose pictures the stains, of mortals' brief time -
Spirits unanswerable haunt with their longings
These breathing remains, with hopes of the Sublime.

In Thanks

Praise be....
For doom-mongering poets
Whose word is not Fate
But meaninglessness on and on...
Who laugh sardonically at
Pity's full attempt to
Make something of
Hearts' broken dreams;
Who break my mind in two
Broken pieces... Because
Leaving them, when I
Face the world again, through
Melancholy then wells
Joy!
Found in fallen nature's
Aching meaning;
Which is poetry.

Praise be....
For the days of grimmer hue;
Whose shades forget sunshine
And stretch out rolled in languid cloud,
Who hide horizons in
Mystery and solitude
And bring forebo
-ding wrapped in gloom.
Who light the eye with soft
Tones of twilight...Because
Bathed in them, all
Quiet things find new life; The
Colours and the strains of
Soul...

Painted by the searching
Heart and conscience,
Which is Truth.

Praise be...
For times of constant trial;
When life seems one long chain
Of petty troubles on and on...
With each new turning fresh
Troubles, minute annoyances
Sting to action the
Whiplash of the tongue;
When duty storms at peace
And sweet pleasure... Because
Through these foils, my
Heart and conscience wake,
Watching once more the road in
Prayer...
Looking for the glimmer
In the darkness
Who is God.

Journey

Along a long, exhausted road,
Where concrete clumps like gallows stand,
Enshelled by steel, through mesh of rain,
And burdened with our baggage load;
We drive, seeking a promised land
Where we shall have a home again.
Each splash of window-warmth reminds,
A word in light still draws us on -
Though signposts vanish without trace
And fuel ebbs - the symbol shone
On memory of the heart that finds
And looks upon a longed-for face.

Liturgical colours

"Mama, why do the colours at Church,
change as the seasons do?"
"Like the seasons, they teach us of life and of death;
help our hearts remain true
to the suffering and joy of the Mother
who makes life and love ever new.
The Church is our mother in Spirit,
as Nature is our body's nurse,
and each daughter of the Creator reflects
the other: rehears-
ing the shades and the glory of being;
God's blessings, and evil's dark curse.

97

Tranquil and vital the green which now clothes
the Earth and the Church, a draught
of visual refreshment to world-weary men,
that they rise and go on to the last.
Our Lady, Mother and Queen of all:
she colours the firmament vast;
above us she reigns, exalted,
chaste as the sun's brilliant light
radiant from clouds of ethereal dew,
lovely and spotlessly white;
blue as the deepest of man's longing dreams
gazing to heaven in his plight.
Crimson the colour for martyrs,
strong as their own precious blood,
poured away, emptied upon the dark earth,
that we may receive mercy's flood;
powerful reminder of graces
bestowed on those raised from the mud.
Golden and glorious, as sunlight,
Royalty's splendour above,
and white, the purest of colours,
innocent as the sweet dove,
containing the light of all others,
stand for our God who is Love.
Purple as twilight's foreboding
are the seasons we watch and we mourn,
lest the darkness steal o'er us unready,
and make us its own, all forlorn;
for dusk is the hour of repentance,
that Christ will be near till the morn.
Unknown is the colour of blackness,
unknown is the fate of a friend:
Glory spurning, in shadows abysmal
Ponderous, proud souls descend;
Flown into orbits of mystery
Love-lighted being finds true end.

Visitation

With lightening leap, the hallowed herald cries
Both life and death, all pain, all joy foretold:
Heaven's Word here upon earth shall soon unfold,
It's lowly echo yet shall reach the skies!
An Infant's hand the world shall overturn:
Humble the proud, uplift the meek and poor;
Bring heaven to earth, unbolt Sheol's dark door;
This spark of life, God's flame, shall soar and burn.
Unborn, the prophet speaks within the womb:
Salvation's light is radiant now in man!
Sign of contention, peaceful as the lamb;
Unblaming witness to innocents' doom.
That bound of life sounds boundless depths of love,
A word for womb-shrined victims from Above.

Patience

Oh Patience! Where? Where is your dwelling place?
Where might I kneel to leave a suppliant word?
Enthroned aloft, in monumental guise,
Surveying rampant crowds with agate eyes?
But you are tender, full of pity's grace;
No mob obeys, no spokesman makes thee heard.
Desire has scorned, Men shunned thy lambent sight;
All but lone victims of the Dreadful Night[7].
Art thou in thrall to some dank jailer's keys,
A pearl of pity in a blackened shell?
With Christ draining the cup unto the lees;
Would that my heart could make me do so well.
But my own soul is cell enough for thee -
Oh queenly servant, hear and come to me!

---

[7]　c.f. James Thomson's 'The City of Dreadful Night' - although the figure of the lady at the end is Melancholia, there is a strong element of patience as a necessary quality to those who wander there which projected itself into my vision of this statuesque beauty.

Lenten Songs

I

Out of my depths I cry to thee O Lord;
Make my voice raise to Thee
A song of heartfelt pleading!
Pent in my soul is the shadow of thy grief,
Heart of my heart dungeoned round by self-set walls;
Lord rend my heart, and give thy Word relief!

Chain me to my sin: I cannot stand,
Weight of offence
Like a millstone with its plunder.
Poised on the brink, bemused I do not plead,
Watching the swell of grey and turgid world,
None but Thy voice can teach me of my need.

Redeem me, Lord, from Complacency;
Forgive, that I in shame
May weep my love upon Thee.
Surer than daybreak is thy mercy's light;
Rouse with its dawn the sleeping soul within me,
So may I cry to Thee with all my might.

II

Pity me, Lord, that I do not pity you,
And make my soul for sorrow keen.
How grief breathes sighs through senseless things,
What tears must be in things unseen;
My plastic heart and painted eyes
Unmoved as Love in torment dies.

Trouble me Lord, as I do not trouble you,
Until you rouse me from my idle sleep.
Birds, villains, knock upon your heaven's door,
And children ponder matters deep;
Assiduous I tread world's wheel;
Spirit's delight - where is my zeal?

Rejoice me Lord, for I know my joy is you;
Let all my being thrill with pure delight.
How high my heart in gratitude is borne,
In sweet resolve to do all things aright!
Yet if more deeply do I love in pain -
Grant me a tender heart to wound again.

Poem on Mass in the Kirks' chapel-like dining room with furnishings rescued from demolished old churches.

The tender curves of wing are delicate with awe,
Love, worship form those hands like votive flame.
Rapt eyes full selves upon the Mystery pour,
And lips which long but dare not speak His name.

So exiled angels kneel before their King,
Who seeks to raise the poor, sick and bereft.
The agèd carvings with new meaning sing,
A wound is healed which Man and Time had cleft.

Here greet Him, blindly, men on earthly trial,
About Him all the hidden heavens throng!
Kirk's spirit hovers with enraptured smile
To see new Heaven with earthly joys belong.

Narcissus and his Followers

"Love, Narcissus, of all joy the root,
 Delight you sowed within the hearts of all,
 Will you alone know nothing of its fruit?
 Narcissus - awake!"

"Peerless image is the good I choose,
 Doting upon this apple of my eye;
 I love a being I can never lose,
 For my ideal's sake."

103

"Have you forgot, how gracious were our days
 When you laughed and strove amongst us still?
 Friendship's light returned your every gaze...
 Narcissus - awake!"

"Glorious dreams, led me to destiny,
 My deeds were in another, shameful, life -
 Friends, foes, all fall before the effigy,
 For my ideal's sake."

"Idolater! You know we shall not bow,
 Or be seduced by ravishing decay.
 Repent or we must turn against you now;
 Narcissus - awake!"

"Your threats and weapons, they can do no harm,
 Touch not the paragon I worship here!
 Its life is mine and both are in a charm
 For my ideal's sake."

"We are beset, with troubles and with grief
 Your countenance and hands once helped us bear;
 Do not forget us, in your self-belief -
 Narcissus - awake!"

"Troubles fade when one forgets to think,
 Lose yourselves in self-fulfilling dream,
 Sit with me and gaze, upon the brink,
 For my ideal's sake."

"You roused regard for beauty not our own
 And now we watch it fade away and die,
 Weep for something we have never known;
 Narcissus - awake!

104

You will not face us? then we face our doom,
  Fading to shadows, echoes of ourselves,
  Selves, all shadows, echoing your doom:
  Narcissus - awake!"

"If I should wake, 'twould be a barren morning:
Cold, grey, still, with hungry eyes upon me;
Should I be myself, unmade and lonely?
Reft from dream all for a jealous warning!
Challenge rise from creatures low and fawning.
Glory fade, this heart it nurtures break -
Still my image I cannot forsake."

106

Simeon

Those shoulders, strung with tension of high hope,
Through heavy years have borne the promise on;
They raise it now in thanks, and then are free.
No longer need his people blindly grope
To find God's way, for He has sent the Son,
The Saviour, here, to His sanctuary.
Valour and might have sounded false alarms -
Messiahs who would stain the Temple red;
This day one aged man gives Him embrace.
We see an infant, stretching tiny arms,
We see the wondering poise of silver head,
Mary and Joseph only watch his face -
For none but they could witness such a sign
Resplendent in his eyes: the Light divine.

108

Inspiration

Dreamland

In a land of gold-grey,
Of rose-beige and cream-green,
In a world of a-symmetry,
Patterned throughout.
In a texture of firm cloud,
A mind-span of mystery,
Immense though in miniature:
Land without bounds;
Where concepts are castles,
Worlds' walls crumble down,
And pictures, like raindrops,
Lie shimmering.

A Walk in the state of Exhaustion

The silent bond of sleep
Bearing between my eyes,
With heavy, sinking, steady pull
Enclosing me within glass walls,
Round which the dark tide creeps;
'Till drowned in velvet black -
My hole of vision fringed
By shattered light and shadow strands;
The narrow picture's coloured sands
Trembling with life night brings -
I sway through a dreamland,
With tingling, aching limbs;
The people of another world
Masquing a message; noises hurled
Weave one wild voice which sings.

Books seen slipping to sleep

Seen from sand-heavy miles away
(The borders of another world)
A tight forest of pillars burn
Their many colours on the mind;
Upright, but with questions soft-curled
About their towering masses, and
'Though of power undoubted,
Challenge strangers with dubious dreams,
Seductive, sinuous before
Those of enquiring turn.

And as, bewitched with heady awe,
My eyes narrowed to pierce the haze
Of shimmering distance, or of
Sorcery; I left my shell behind
To dart toward them, hypnotized
And find the land of mystery – to
Which they, surely, guardians stood –
They changed their shape in subtle ways:
Advanced, retired and flickered round;
Played with imagination, beckoned;
Froze and turned to spines.

A Secret Life

Behind those double doors steadfastly closed,
She entertains my love with visions rare,
Enchanting; fascinates with questions posed.
What dreams weaves she before his thirsting eyes?
What does she offer him that I know not?
How does her soul lift him beyond the skies?
Her voice as water deep, as air is soft;
Her touch a fresh caress, thrilling to life;
Her words, my husband says, soar far aloft.
The thoughts she wakes in him are potent spells,
To draw him ever from me to her side,
To that closed sanctuary where she dwells.
Nor shall I vie with her, my love to keep;
Dark is her power, and her name is Sleep.

Insomniac

Sleeplessness is the gift of the Gods –
To grasp time, spin it out
In golden threads of silence;
Watch the languid hours arcing
In slow motion, thrown through space;
Allotted, stolen, and how prized,
But not wasted, no; fading
As the sparkling silt in paced-past sands.

114

To live another life,
Energized, with nerves afire.
To blaze a trail of dream's
Activities! To be another being
Your own self, in the after-world
Of darkling electric senses;
Brave the phantom thoughts in conscious mind.

To cheat grey harpie Time;
Stay up, carouse with secret-sweet,
Surreptitious, gleeful laughter,
Though her stern brows beat a gaze
Of prophecy, dragging all life
Behind her – See new vistas -
Hovering on wings of wakeful hours.

And once in a blue-moon,
Witness the stately dance of
Night, coyly slipping her
Veil from clandestine stars...a
Sight paid for in human breath, drawn,
Gasped away to weave the
Evening breezes, weft with lovers' soul.

But once a while I fear,
Trembling on brimming poise
Of fevered stillness; dazed
By the wild visions of
Blessed, tortured Psyche: For
Sleeplessness is the gift of the
Gods – and those the Gods love die young.

The Drunkard

Eyes gleam-full as dream-bleared moonstones,
Grin as wide as his gaping wish to please,
With tongue-tripped art, drawing his story-sketch
Like a present from a child's treasure-chest:

Thunder's tirades shake his fist and voices,
Clouds of cunning steal his sunshine's stage.
Characters of children's fairytales for him live
In power which no innocence would give.

The highest tower he climbs is an illusion,
His humblest hideaway a threatened hole;
Washbuckling quests to find peace his past knew,
Helped by annihilation's troubling brew.

Inspiration unattained.

Caught in a breath of bright inspired joy,
My mind vibrates with thronging of winged words
Sent coursing by the spirit's jubilee, a
Flight towards exquisite beauty here.

Riotous, expressions swift ascend,
Convolving pinions blaze, dissolve and fall
Like Icarus from vaunting ecstasy, to
Perish in a brumal, silent sea;

116

Or, confined, feathery velocity
Ever deflected, flit a measured round,
Bright eyes reflecting heavens beyond reach
Their instinct knows and longs, and longs, to teach.

How can my open eyes imbibe in joy,
Tranquil, while caged love-birds beat within?
Each blessed draught of sweet inoculation
Darkens pain of heart-breaking clipped wings.

Creative Block (Or: Song of the Hermit-Crab Shell)

I'm
like a
hermit-crab
shell:Hollow, dis-
carded by the life that
once was live in me –
A splendid creature dreamed
in vivid extra-sanity; a
rose-tinted stirring, sad-eyed
tentaculous enquiry waving at the
world; a cornet of ideas, form so strange
as to re-dream life to mad picturesque
unknown sense, when it revealed itself;
Tender and soft, sea-changing. Ready
with its wit-sharp, razor claws if attacked;
beauteous curiosity which made a home
of my mind, treasure vault of my heart.
Then left me: my creative soul.
Now all that I have force to do,
if you hold me close, and
listen very carefully, is
mourn a tune, with
borrowed breath
that I *was*
live.

Poetic Self

Who has awakened me?
I know that you are I -
But in a dream I fell to sleep,
And now awake I am adream -
My breathe your sigh.

Who is it calling me?
A voice was in the air -
And through my veins its singing plays
A moment, speaking of always,
Nor lingers there.

Who shall become of me?
For as I speak, they live -
For vivid instants of a world -
But vanish ere 'tis all unfurled;
My life I give.

Looking Up. (A marching ditty for London).

When you trundle through the city,
Like a cog in a machine,
Breathing monsters' exhalations,
Bearing fumers' exhortations,
Seeing shop-fronts that you wish you hadn't seen;
Pause to feel a moments pity
For your fellows trapped below
- Then look up!

Up above the gleary windows,
And the business-driven men,
Is an ancient world that lingers,
Built by art and loving fingers,
A memorial to the beauty that has been;
Where the dignity within glows
Through harmonious forms without,
Looking up.

Noble souls betrayed by fashion
To a gaudy, gross display,
Decorated and degraded;
So these palaces, now faded,
Deck themselves in modern commerce, light and cheap;
But above these rags a passion
Wrote its tale in gracious lines,
Looking up.

Gentle arches soothe sore eyes there
With eternal brooding peace,
Heavy minds leap with light towers,
Sore hearts touch those carved flowers,
Scrolls and statues tell small men of matters deep.
And the spires which brush the skies there
Raise tired earth-bound souls to heaven,
Looking up.

Centuries have nursed and reared
Throngs of men and monuments;
Restless urban spirits' harbour,
Strongholds of undying ardour,
From each age a character of stone lives on;
Memories to love or fear,
Speak to eyes open to hear,
Looking up.

Looking Down

This grimy pavement exudes subtle joy
And consolation from its rugged face;
No stars or suns could spell out such a trace
Of home and eulogistic memory
As unmoving, it tosses like a toy,
Into the air, for mind to catch and hold
With tingling nerves, and grateful heart enfold;
Less sought, more prized, a gift could rarely be.

Perhaps I look too often at the ground;
I plead excuse, at least in urban ways:
There eyes are quiet, and vision breaks the haze
Of mental fog, whilst pace the patient feet
Upon their patterned, perfectly planned round.
And whilst in refuge at some place within,
The scents, the colours osmosize one's skin,
That I should know them, if again we meet.

The bland and cracked pavements of London South -
Where I once skipped and jumped, careless and free,
Though all the world was rules, or mystery;
Or stalked excited, nervous limbs athrill,
Back taut, head high, and heart within my mouth;
Ambled sometimes, discoursing with friends,
Feet driven as each tone or thought commends -
The moods, if not the days, are there at will.

The dark and mossy streets of Chorleywood,
Where roads seemed to breathe easy, as did I,
Beneath the sunnier, starrier sky;
Where houses made of home-making an art;
And sylvan things crept softly from the wood
To lure the wanderer another mile
Into their cool embrace, with charming guile.

Such pine-strewn, muddy lanes renew my heart.

Broad slabs of gray, as calm as sky and sea
At peace - and quite as old they feel in truth -
St. Andrews paves the way for all its youth:
Who paint the town by night and sleep by day,
With all their jesting, love its dignity,
Its stones which speak of things deeper than time,
And where there seems no reason, give a rhyme -
The lanes which might have set me on my way.

Lancaster's porous rock of many hues -
Rainbows appear for paths after the rain
To make lorn treasure hunters think again!
Before them streams a flood of rosy gold
As though the sun with life the stone imbues,
And mounting up towards the lovely height,
Or moseying beside the river bright,
The new life there but graces all the old.

People once claimed London paved with gold-
A city royal where fortune bowed to fame;
There hopeful seekers looking for a name
Found honour was more fickle than she seems
And wisdom does not wait upon the bold;
They settled for a seat of filigree.
No city proud, no road is gold to me,
But many humble routes are paved with dreams.

Personification

Solitude often purls, like a feline wandering lost
Around my ankles; pleading sweet water of time,
To turn to diamonds in its cool, eternal eyes.
Smokily it wreathes into distance, trailing still
A tattered robe of schemes it might have blessed.

Happiness comes leaping out to meet me like a child,
Radiant, bursting, with the light of joyous news,
Or the music of a great achievement sung.
Gracefully you'll see her golden head bowed in the sun,
Reading memories sweet or tender love confessed.

Inspiration is the goddess all men eagerly implore,
Fickle Mistress, benefactress, noble Muse;
The fairy midwife of all glorious dreams.
Her daughters are the shapely models of all human arts,
No mind nor spirit they have ne'er caressed.

Pragmatism glowers, left behind by Poetry
Flown in rapture; still he paces on his guard
Lest the ugly Facts should burst through Time's neat bars.
Impatience capers witchlike, knowing gleams her one eye,
And her telescopic claws the keep contest!

Patience strews her flowers and tears over her friends,
Who lie embalmed by Hope, 'till promised Dawn
Shall blow his argent bugle's rising call;
His chariot of stars, all new life in his train,
Or and incarnadine his vaulting crest.

Humility's a songbird living in the bosky shade,
Observing bright eyed all the daylit world;
Her glee outpoured flows as eternal prayer.
Pride lurks like a vulture, pinions, claws of pitch and flame,
To claim and savage good we once possessed.

Reason is the judge with eyes of fire 'back of his head -
All appeal to him, but none can see him clear -
For his form's from tangled intricacies made.
Lo! Human Nature's trillion faces tower tall,
Yet she's known in urchin's grasp or mother's breast.

Love is adored and hated by the children of this world;
Is killed, yet lives, truly, eternally -
Whilst His name is mocked by Venus and her boy:
Her beauty or his arrows pierce the roving eye,
Still Love in passion to the cross is pressed.

Like a Maple

He rises like a maple tree aglow
In autumn, herald of the dying year:
A splendour blent of ecstasy and fear
For truth we feel and mystery we know.
Pure gold of sun bright: myriad leaves rejoice
And paint a glory to the gift of sight;
True blood, the hearts' life, seems to show its might:
Deep scarlet glows and gives passion a voice.
Though pent by freezing strictures of the dark,[8]
Sun's influence makes spring the shooting sap
Leaping to life 'neath heaven's radiant arc,
A gush of sweetness, joy sprung from mishap.
So then is born, through strife of fire and frost,
A vital nectar; no travail is lost.

---

[8] The sweet maple tree is unique in a system which functions in the opposite way to other plant's methods of circulating, ingesting and exuding liquid, sap etc. When the frost comes, it freezes the sap within the tree; in the heat of the thaw, sudden change of pressure sends the syrup shooting up along the trunk and limbs of the tree and it pours out of any holes therein, whereby men harvest it.

A Sonnet to a Sonnet
(dedicated to Miriam)

A sonnet to a sonnet I shall sing -
A song of joy to free the lightsome year
Now fled: your airy sweetness gave it wing,
And to my heart a tune and rhythm more clear.
Exquisitely compact, perfectly small;
A meld harmonious of tempers extreme:
You dance, gleeful, you climb, nor fear to fall,
Yet cling to me for hours in some soft dream.
The sage knows only that he cannot say
What Time may bring, wrapt in her obscure cloak;
With glittering prophecy I shall not yoke
My daughter, on this early, happy, day.
But sonnet-like, the sparkle in your eyes,
Bids us hold breath for some future surprise.

Shadows

Shadow is but reflection in a mystic glass -
The dull, uneven mirror of the earth.
To clouded view its play is only farce,
The wise regard beholds a cryptic birth:
There squat the shrunken goblins at your feet,
Here emanate the eleven figures tall;
With quivering magic silhouettes replete
Cut sprightly capers, or like serpents crawl.
Do they have life and power of their own?
Or does Apollo conjure from each soul
A phantom, whispering whence it has grown,
Shade eloquent through occult, mimic role?
In potentia stencilled what may be -
So dark, so light, so small, so great are we.

Untitled Sonnet

This age has lost its soul in reams of prose;
The law of lawlessness despises form:
Who breathes a sigh over the fading rose?
Who is so maudlin as to fear a storm?
The poem becomes Political Complaint,
Word of the cult of cultlessness, so free
It has no god but Self, no guiding saint –
No star but Individuality.
Yet if I breathe the rhythm of a dance,
Flowing from arcane springs o'er my new tongue,
My unique sense of life will not entrance,
But scorn hurl at the vision I have sung.
Is there, in truth, Poetry left to write? –
Its music floats like stars through this dark night.

Appendix

Haven't you noticed?
Nowadays the critic is the artist.
The artist presents a pile of rubbish
for the critic to have the honour
of exegesis on - imaginative catharsis.
So; in your capable mind,
I leave this work.

Also from Saint Austin Press …

Eilein na h-Òige: The Poems of Fr Allan McDonald

Edited by Ronald Black

Crom mun t-saogh'l, gur sèimh an oidhch'
Mar mhàthair ri faire chloinn fo shuain;
Sèimhe d'uchd-sa, 'Mhoire mhìn,
'Tàladh Chrìost' 's do chridh' ri 'ghruaidh.

Crouched round the world, the night is gentle
Like a mother watching her children sleep;
More gentle's Your bosom, O lovely Mary,
As You lullaby Christ with Your heart to His cheek.

Fr Allan McDonald (1859-1905), priest, poet and folklorist, is one of the best-loved pastors the Scottish Catholic church has ever known. His name is evergreen in the Gaelic-speaking islands of South Uist, Barra and Eriskay, where he is remembered simply as *Maighstir Ailein* - Father Allan. A native of Fort William, trained for the priesthood at Blairs and Valladolid, he wore himself out in the service of his parishioners at Daliburgh in South Uist. In 1894 he was transferred to Eriskay, his beloved 'Isle of Youth', where he built the fine church that can be seen today.

Fr Allan was a legend in his own lifetime. He inspired the characters of "Fr MacCrimmon" in Frederic Breton's *Heroine in Homespun* (1893) and "Fr Ludovic" in Neil Munro's *Children of the Tempest* (1903), becoming himself again in Amy Murray's *Father Allan's Island* (1936). A still more remarkable series of books was to follow, however. The late Dr John Lorne Campbell of Canna published his biography in 1956 (*Fr Allan McDonald of Eriskay*), his lexicographical work in 1958 (*Gaelic Words and Expressions from South Uist and Eriskay*), his manuscript poetry in 1965 (*Bàrdachd Mhgr Ailein*) and his collection of stories of the supernatural in 1968 (*Strange Things*). But his priceless collection of general Gaelic folklore lies largely unpublished in the library of Edinburgh University.

Amongst Fr Allan's heroic labours was the publication in 1893 of a Gaelic Hymnal. A Presbyterian minister wrote of it in 1894, "Several of the hymns in this collection are his own composition and seem to me to be very beautiful." Dr Campbell identified altogether eighteen items which Fr Allan had composed himself.

In this new anthology, Ronald Black has brought these eighteen hymns together with sixteen religious poems from *Bàrdachd Mhgr Ailein* and provided facing English translations. The result is an exciting and lyrical celebration of Catholic faith, full of the clear vision of a dedicated pastor and the unique atmosphere of the Western Isles. Dr Campbell's biography of 1956 is also reprinted with additional material, while in a brief introductory essay the editor, Ronald Black, assesses Fr Allan's contribution to Gaelic literature.

Ronald Black, formerly Senior Lecturer in Celtic in Edinburgh University, is Gaelic Editor of *The Scotsman* and of the Uist community newspaper *Am Pàipear*. Among his other publications are *An Tuil: Anthology of 20th Century Scottish Gaelic Verse* (Polygon, 1999), *Smuaintean fo Éiseabhal: Thoughts under Easaval*, the poetry of Dòmhnall Aonghais Bhàin of South Uist (Birlinn, 2000), and *An Lasair: Anthology of 18th Century Scottish Gaelic Verse* (Birlinn, 2001).

Eilein na h-Òige: The Poems of Fr Allan McDonald, **edited by Ronald Black.**
Paperback. ISBN 1 901157 61 X.
£14.95 ; $26.95 in the U.S.A.

Published by Mungo Books, an imprint of The Saint Austin Press.

www.saintaustin.org

The Book of Christian Classics

Edited with an Introduction by Michael Williams

For two thousand years, Christianity has informed and inspired a multitude of great writers. The relationship between the Catholic faith and literature is a profound and even necessary one, for it is the Word Incarnate Who is the Creator of all things and the object of our worship. Christ is the fullness of God's revelation of Himself to man, the centre of human history, *tenens medium in omnibus*. It is He, therefore, Who lies at the centre of that tradition of literary endeavour which is presented here.

Like the "scribe of the kingdom...who bringeth forth from his treasure new things and old" (Matt. 13:52), this anthology brings together in one volume a selection of some of the best of Christian devotional writing, spanning two millennia from the Fathers of the Church to the early twentieth century.

The Book of Christian Classics, edited with an introduction by Michael Williams.
466 pages, clothbound with ribbon. ISBN 1 901157 21 0.
£12.95 ; $27.50 in the U.S.A.

Published by The Saint Austin Press.

www.saintaustin.org

Beyond the Blue Glass, Volume I

Catholic Essays on Faith and Culture

Aidan Nichols OP

The first of two volumes of dazzling essays on faith and culture by one of the most gifted and erudite Catholic thinkers today. The range and depth of these essays is remarkable, covering many of the most significant themes and theologians of the twentieth century: liturgy, literature, the Anglican "Radical Orthodoxy" movement, Scheeben, Newman and, of course, St Thomas. What is particularly impressive about this collection is the way in which Nichols presents us with a panoramic sweep in which clarity, detail and sobriety are not sacrificed to scope and virtuosity. No one interested in the major issues of modern theology will want to miss this book.

Essays include:

- St Thomas in His Time

- Thomism and the *Nouvelle Théologie*

- Balthasar and Rahner: "Anonymous Christianity" in Question

- Cardinal Ratzinger on Theology, Liturgy and Faith

- A Tale of Two Documents: *Sacrosanctum Concilium* and *Mediator Dei*

- Liturgy as Consummate Philosophy: A Reading of Pickstock's *After Writing*

"Father Aidan Nichols is the most prolific and versatile English Catholic theologian of his generation. He deserves a high place of honour in that Dominican Gallery *of which he is himself the historian."*

Professor John Saward

Fr Aidan Nichols, O.P., is the Prior of Blackfriars, Cambridge, and author of some twenty-five books, including Dominican Gallery, The Shape of Catholic Theology, The Theology of Joseph Ratzinger: An Introductory Study *and the forthcoming* Discovering Aquinas.

Beyond the Blue Glass, Volume I, by Aidan Nichols OP. 210 pages, clothbound. ISBN 1 901157 16 4. £14.95 ; $26.95 in the U.S.A.

Published by The Saint Austin Press.

www.saintaustin.org

Printed in Great Britain
by Amazon